TIDES OF CHANGE

PHOTOGRAPHY BY RICK GOLT

WRITTEN BY BOB KRAUSS

ISLAND HERITAGE PUBLISHING
A division of The Madden Corporation

HAWAII, TIDES OF CHANGE™

Photography by Rick Golt
Written by Bob Krauss

Copyright © 1989 by
Island Heritage Publishing
A Division of The Madden Corporation
99-880 Iwaena Street
Aiea, Hawaii 96701
(808) 487-7299

Second Printing—1990

ISBN 0-89610-160-6
Printed in Hong Kong

Editor, Penny Pence Smith
Design and Art Direction, Bud Linschoten
Jacket Design, Paul Turley
Project Director, Dixon J. Smith

CONTENTS

North Shore, Oahu

Tides of Change

Tides of change have swept our islands since the first eruption of fire and smoke and ashes emerged from the deep stillness perhaps seventy million years ago. *Pele,* the goddess of volcanoes, is erratic change herself; fickle, jealous, violent, and destructive of those she loves. So the islands grew in sporadic, compulsive, upwelling change.

Other forces of change immediately set to work. Great ocean swells, with a momentum unhindered for two thousand miles, broke in unceasing rhythm upon the upstart islands, patiently grinding the jagged edges of lava to smoothness. In an epic battle of the gods, lava exploded as it surged into the ocean and, lo, within a week or two, there was a graceful black sand beach. Within a century or two, lava devoured the beach and all was changed again.

The islands rose and subsided beneath the sea and rose again into the mists of the sky and fickle *Pele* moved on to create and destroy some different place. Other gods brought wind and rain and clouds and thunder. They frolicked on the mountain tops while the waters of *Kane* gouged chasms and sharpened ridges and continued the slow, constant process of change. The gods played and made love amid the craters and cinder cones grown cold, smoothing the edges with caresses, investing the silence with *mana,* the spirit force, waiting for life.

Life arrived on the storm-driven wind, high above in the jet stream, clinging to the wings of migrating birds, stuck in the mud at their feet, drifting on the endless sea; seeds, eggs, nettles, spores, birds, insects, plants, even a mammal, the bat. They arrived with agonizing slowness, the establishment of each new life form measured in hundreds of milleniums. All the while weather and the ocean, those unceasing forces of change, imprinted their wills upon the helpless, fragile islands.

But the islands also have a will of their own. They began to change the living things that came to them. These changes were not capricious. They were responses by life forms to the new rules imposed by the islands. So, while the islands were being changed, they also effected changes that startle students of scientific disciplines. By comparison with changes imposed *upon* the islands, the changes imposed *by* the islands are probably more subtle, less understood and the most intriguing.

The tiny fruit fly proliferated into hundreds of species that attract mates as no fruit flies ever courted before. Two species of birds and many more insects lost their ability to fly. Stickery plant pods that stowed away to the islands by clinging to the wings of birds grew plants that eventually lost their stickers. Among the best known adapters to survival on the islands are land snails. More species of land snails evolved in Hawaii than in the entire continental United States.

One of the island adaptations has been called, for want of a more scientific description, "loss of competitiveness." Tree bark that was bitter in other lands sweetened in

Hawaii. Poisonous plants that migrated to the islands lost their poison. There are good reasons for this. Poison and bitterness in plants can be an evolutionary response to being eaten by grazing animals. Since there were no grazing animals in Hawaii before European discovery, the plants did not need to produce poison to protect themselves.

In a competitive world, the lack of competitiveness among plants in early Hawaii is one of the fascinating aspects of island biology. It has been proposed that each new immigrant began its career as a "weed" aggressively occupying new territory. But somehow, for many and specific reasons including small space, the ferocity of the plants subsided and they became less aggressive than their mainland cousins.

So, factors that effected change *by* the islands were already in operation when the first voyaging canoe appeared on the horizon less than two thousand years ago. The hardy, seagoing Polynesians in the canoe gradually drew into focus those factors that would influence their own lives as they had on the islands from which these immigrants came.

For one thing, after a voyage of probably three weeks, they were aware of their isolation in space. Also, the offshore view of their new world told them that they had found an island of a size they could grasp in their minds. In this they were modern. For thousands of years, other humans had led camels through endless deserts, ridden shaggy ponies across vast steppes, walked behind oxen over far reaching plains to form the concept of a limitless world to be conquered.

It was not until the space age when a photo, taken of our island earth from a satellite, demonstrated the small size of our world, its limitations and its isolation in space. The global village may be a new concept to continents but it has always been a fact of life in the islands.

The newly arrived Polynesians certainly were aware of another factor that would influence their behavior on the island, their vulnerability to one another. Survival within the confines of their canoe had depended more upon cooperation than competition. The isolation of their new world, its small size and its limitations would simply act as a somewhat larger canoe. As the population increased and each valley became occupied, there was no escape without leaving the planet. They must learn to get along with one another.

These Polynesian immigrants could not have been born with a specialized talent for survival on islands. They must have learned to adapt and to evolve a culture based on these adaptations, much as plants developed new species by adapting. Some of their adaptations would appear to be naive, almost childlike. The Hawaiian method of warfare, for example, appears to be more sport than combat. Battles frequently broke out but seldom lasted for more than a few days and armies stopped fighting to rest at night. Sometimes the outcome was decided by individual competition, like a heavyweight championship boxing match, between a fighter from either camp.

Heroic legends speak of great numbers slaughtered in these wars. Hard evidence is more modest. Captain James Cook, who discovered the Hawaiian Islands for Western Civilization, returned to Kauai in 1779 shortly after a revolution which passed power from one ruling chief to another. Cook reported that the dead numbered three chiefs and twenty-four commoners. Warriors still nursing injuries and showing the scars of battle visited Cook's ship. These numbers demonstrate how the Hawaiians were able to wage war for more than a thousand years and still survive, even increase in population. On close inspection, then, the island method of limited warfare appears quite sophisticated considering casualties suffered during the U.S. Civil War and other "civilized" combat.

Much of the excitement of warfare in ancient Hawaii came from diplomatic maneuver, from pre-battle bluster and taunting of the enemy. A major expenditure of wealth and energy for war went into restoring war temples or building new temples to the war gods because the best way to win a war, or at least avoid one, was to convince the enemy that one's own war god was invincible. Expenditures on today's war temples, called weapons systems, a heavy reliance on deterrence, and the number of limited wars being fought on our island Earth today all bear striking similarities to old island adaptations.

Hawaiians evolved the *Makahiki,* another practical technique to limit the destructiveness of warfare. During a period in the winter when storm seas made invasions of neighboring islands hazardous, the god of war, *Ku,* relinquished his pre-eminence temporarily to *Lono,* god of peace and agriculture. Inhabitants of the islands were under a *kapu* during this period to remain within the confines of their land divisions, a restriction which effectively prevented military campaigns. The period during which *Lono* ruled was a time for sporting events, hula performances, feasts and payment of taxes. We know that the *Makahiki* was practiced into historical times because Captain Cook arrived during this season and was mistaken for *Lono*.

If such a concept was institutionalized today, it would require a global cessation of hostilities once a year for two to three weeks. This would be a time for holding The Olympic Games, international arts and crafts, dance and literary competitions, fairs, feasts and festivals and religious observances all over the world. At the same time, everyone would rededicate themselves to national sovereignties.

One other island adaptation concerning cleanliness and waste disposal deserves mention in view of our modern preoccupation with the problems caused by nuclear, chemical, industrial, human and other forms of pollution. A man named Townsend, supercargo of the *Neptune,* wrote in 1798, "They (Hawaiians) certainly are the most cleanly people that I have ever seen." His observation about cleanliness among pre-contact Hawaiians is confirmed by others and at least one modern study has been made of the subject. Living so near the ocean with daily opportunities to bathe may account for this concern for cleanliness.

But cleanliness in old Hawaii went beyond bathing. The people of old took waste disposal seriously. Food scraps, human feces, hair cuttings, fingernail clippings, cast off *malos* (loin cloths) and other personal waste had to be disposed of carefully because these items contained a spark of *mana* or spiritual force. Attendants of chiefs carried spittoons for the careful disposal of royal body waste. Were a *kahuna anaana* (witch doctor) to obtain a piece of one's waste, containing a spark of one's *mana,* he would have the bait used to pray you to death. So the penalty for careless disposal of waste in the islands was severe.

During the same period, Captain Nathaniel Portlock, a fur trader on the North-west Coast of America who also visited Hawaii, reported in 1787 that one of his men remained among the Indians for three days and they seemed fond of his company although the sailor was offended by their habit of throwing food scraps into a corner of their hut. At the same time, this tribe of Northwest Indians had plenty of space and were quite mobile, moving frequently from place to place in their canoes. Waste could simply be left behind. Hawaiians did not have this luxury in their limited space as we no longer do in ours.

With the arrival of explorers and fur traders, Hawaii was no longer remote in space. Limitations to outside resources were removed. The newcomers brought iron, muskets, cloth, cattle, horses, new plants and so many other novelties that our focus shifts again to the changes acting *upon* the islands. Within forty years, this tidal wave of change overwhelmed the old gods who presided over limited resources. The new king, son of the old warrior chief, rejected the old gods.

There followed a wholesale abolishment of long accepted limitations as foreign wealth flooded in. Merchants brought a new economy. In 1820 American missionaries brought a new God. Whale ships brought a new source of income that increased to undreamed dimensions with the success of a crop called sugar cane which the old Hawaiians had planted alongside their taro patches. Annexation to the United States in 1898 created boom times and more change, to be magnified by Statehood in 1959. By this time, Hawaii had become the exotic extension of a continent as well as an island isolated in space.

Yet the subtle, persuasive, carrot and stick inducements of the islands to change people continued in operation. From first contact, the combination of exotic appeal and economic opportunity in the islands attracted new residents of wildly various persuasions. Sailors deserted their ships and stayed. Adventurers turned stopovers into careers. Foreign consul generals often forgot to go home. A need for labor in the sugar cane fields brought newcomers of all races and nationalities; Chinese, Portuguese, Germans, Norwegians, Japanese, Filipinos, Koreans. Each group came with its own identity and culture to be gradually transformed into something different.

Hawaiians took sea chanties and Protestant hymns and turned them into island music. A small Portuguese guitar became the ukulele. Hawaii's dismaying cacophony of languages merged into expressive *pidgin*. The missionary mother hubbard was transformed into the *muumuu*. The same inventiveness half a century later gave birth to a colorful creation called the aloha shirt. Grown men with origins as widely separated as Canton and Cleveland learned to wear flowers around their necks. The most startling change came about in babies. They began to be born with the most incredible combinations of racial and cultural background, the ultimate adaptation of men and women who must learn to get along together on an island.

And always there were visitors. Before steamer schedules and the transcontinental railroad, a trip to Hawaii was like going to the moon; six months one way around Cape Horn. Even after, books by authors who visited Hawaii—Mark Twain, Isabella Bird, Robert Louis Stevenson—were as much adventure as travel. But the ingredients were already in place; warm sun and rainbows, tropical scenery with palm trees, friendly and exotic natives, the magnificent spectacle of a live volcano. The jet airplane has cut travel time to Hawaii from Los Angeles to less than five hours and has transformed Waikiki into a forest of high rise luxury hotels.

And so the tides of change continue to run in opposing directions. More than ever, Hawaii is battered by outside forces which change the landscape, the way people think, the way they live on the islands, the way they spend their leisure. It would seem that these tiny, fragile islands must be drowned in a global flood of competing cultures, high technology and economic competition. This is a major concern of thinking people in Hawaii as has been, in the past, a gloomy assessment that the Hawaiian race must eventually become extinct.

But the Hawaiian culture has shown amazing resilience in a boundless sea of change. It is like the pinpoints of the islands in a vast ocean, battered by the endless ranks of swells that beat upon their shores. At these small collision points the swells bend and wrap around the islands. It was this new alignment of the waves that the Polynesian navigators felt in their buttocks as they approached, telling them the islands were ahead.

And it is the same kind of modest message that proclaims the presence of Hawaii to the world today; photos taken on Waikiki Beach in family albums all over the globe, Hawaiian music broadcast by disc jockeys, colorful shirts worn at back yard barbecues, memories of the hula, a recognition of aloha as the universal word for love, hello and goodbye, glossy color photos of Hawaiian beaches and palms trees in advertisements.

These are merely the signposts of a unique identity, like cross currents on the ocean swells. They simply inform the world that here are islands and the message is one of escape. But to learn from and to be changed by the islands is not escape, it is survival. By coincidence, the globe has also become a tiny island isolated in space, limited in resources; an island on which we are all vulnerable to one another. Whether we survive on this island may depend on how well we learn to adapt. So the subtle, little understood forces that effect change *by* islands are rippling out in ever wider scope. The tides of change have only begun.

Sunrise over Olomana, Oahu

Heiau near Wailuku, Maui

Waimea Canyon, Kauai

Volcanoes National Park, Hawaii

Leeward Oahu

Surf at Bamboo Reef, Oahu

Near Halona Point, Oahu

Volcanoes National Park, Hawaii

Sliding sands, Haleakala Crater, Maui

Devastation Trail, Volcanoes National Park, Hawaii

Volcanoes National Park, Hawaii

Heiau, Maui

Kona, Hawaii

Heiau near Aiea, Oahu

Heiau near Wailuku, Maui

Oahu, Hawaii

The Ocean

When someone living in Hawaii suggests, "Let's go to the beach today," it can mean many different things; a family picnic, a ride on a surf board, a fishing expedition, an afternoon date for sunbathing, a hunt for sea shells, an invigorating swim, or a hike along the seashore. The choice of activity determines which beach to visit because there are beaches for each activity, as there are restaurants that specialize in different foods. For example, there are 1,600 recognized surfing sites in the Hawaiian Islands.

So the average islander becomes somewhat sophisticated about beaches as well as the ocean without thinking much about it. The ocean is the common denominator of island life, the subliminal yardstick against which economic decisions are measured, a cohesive ingredient of society as well as the definition of the island itself. The ocean affects so many aspects of our lives that we simply accept it as being there.

Few people on islands bother to ask themselves philosophical questions like, is the ocean an enemy or a friend? Is it a highway or a barrier? Is it a limitation or a resource? That is why early Polynesian navigators set out on incredible voyages without worrying that they might sail off the edge of the world. There is no evidence that such a dilemma ever occurred to them. They were sailors and the ocean was their back yard. Does an astronaut worry about flying off the edge of space?

Most islanders do not philosophize about their beaches, either, until somebody blocks access to them. Or builds a sea wall to the water. Then there are letters to the editor, public hearings and cries of outrage. By long tradition, beaches in Hawaii to the line of vegetation above the sand are public domain. They do not belong to luxury resorts nor to seaside estates, but to anyone who has a use for the beach.

Beaches are windows to the ocean, to the freedom of open space on a small island where space is limited. Beaches are also an opportunity for a fresh start twice every twenty-fours with the slate wiped clean after the high tide washes away untidy evidence of previous occupation. This must be one reason Hawaii's beaches are so inviting to visitors. They offer a rare opportunity to make the first footprint in a tawny, pristine carpet of tropical wilderness.

Children of the islands have the greatest talent for using the ocean and its seashore with resourcefulness and imagination. To a small child, sand is an art medium for sculpture, tidepools an undersea adventure, beach litter the materials for games created on the spot. To children of all ages the ocean is a benediction, a happy rite of spontaneous worship where all who enter here are invited to splash, swim and surf. If baptism is a cleansing, a washing away of sins, then the children of the islands are baptized every time they plunge into the ocean for they come out dripping, grinning, clean, refreshed and whole.

The early Hawaiians recognized such a religious relationship with the ocean and institutionalized it through nature gods, a relationship which offended missionaries. They were particularly critical of a sport which most clearly expressed the old Hawaiian intimacy with and love for the ocean, surfing. Surfing is an embrace of the ocean. To ride the slope of a wave is not to conquer but to communicate, a form of worship.

Protestant missionaries did not believe in what we today call professional sports, and surfing in old Hawaii was certainly a professional sport. *Heiaus* were dedicated to it and chiefs engaged in surfing contests on which there was heavy betting. All of this was much too modern for Puritan values. Missionaries, in their earnest and well meaning attempts to confer upon Hawaiians the blessings of civilization, equated surfing with the sins of frivolity and nudity. They were not yet island people.

To an islander, then, the ocean has never been an enemy but a respected friend. It is not a threat but a blessing. And it is a barrier only in the sense that distance is a barrier. For the ocean is also a highway. The old Polynesians have been called the greatest explorers in history because there are few if any pinpoints of land in the vast Pacific that they did not find. They were avid travelers between islands. Captain Cook, whose men had infected women on Kauai with syphilis in 1778, was startled to find traces of the disease less than one year later on the opposite end of the island chain.

So the islands of the 50th State have a maritime heritage that is unique in the nation because it begins at least one thousand years before Columbus discovered the Americas. First the voyaging canoe, then the square-rigged sailing ship, then the steamer brought overwhelming change. The discovery of Honolulu Harbor in 1794 gave birth to Hawaii's major city and permanently changed the political relationships of Oahu to the other islands. *Alika,* the oldest Hawaiian song that deals with a foreign subject, is about a single-masted ship.

During these years, the biggest continuing story in Honolulu newspapers dealt with ship arrivals. Ships brought fresh news, the latest styles, the first bicycle, the first typewriter, the first tennis racquet, the first golf club, the first automobile. Ships brought toys for Christmas, mills for the plantations, sofas for the parlor, toilet paper for the bathroom. To these fly specks of islands, ships brought whole circuses to entertain children in Honolulu, and landed the circus animals by whale boat on the neighbor islands. Ship arrivals signalled new theatrical seasons, shifts in foreign policy and hordes of new immigrants who spoke foreign tongues.

Ship arrivals were so important to the community that the editor of the weekly *The Polynesian* in the 1840s announced them as news while charging to insert notices of marriage because marriage was, after all, a private affair. Ship arrivals were so vital to the economy of the islands that the Hawaiian government erected a semaphore signal station on Kaimuki Hill. Each vessel in the interisland fleet as well as each important ship from foreign ports had its own semaphore signal which residents of Honolulu recognized as readily as football players respond to signals from the quarterback. A satellite semaphore atop a newspaper building on Merchant Street relayed the signals to the town.

When the semaphore arms moved, merchants sent drays to the waterfront to pick up cargo. Residents got dressed to greet arriving relatives. The pilot boat sailed out and news boats raced off port in stiff competition to be the first on board to pick up the latest foreign newspapers that the captain always purchased just before setting sail. This was the wire service of the day. In 1875 a signal came during Sunday evening service. Ministers obligingly cut short their sermons. Parishioners raced to the dock while the pilot lit the channel buoy lanterns. Everybody waited in the dark until they discovered that the signal had been a mistake.

It is no accident that "boat day" became Honolulu's most colorful institution with a history as unique as it was exciting at the time. Departures of King Kalakaua or other members of the royal family brought crowds to the dock and the Royal Hawaiian Band to serenade the king. Eventually, the band attended every important ship arrival and departure because it was good for business. Flower lei sellers gathered in increasing numbers. Hack drivers lined up for fares.

The monarchy ended and Hawaii became a Territory of the United States before the golden era of the luxury liner arrived. Ships no longer brought the latest news but rather new crops of tourists and infusions of wealth to a growing visitor industry. The Royal Hawaiian Band still sounded the strains of *Aloha Oe,* lei sellers lined the pier sheds and taxi drivers jostled for position. Arriving or departing, streamers floated from ship to dock and everybody became infected with the magic of Hawaii. Boat day held such a nostalgic place in the hearts of islanders that it survived three decades into the era of air travel.

Today most visitors to Hawaii arrive by jet liner, but ocean highways remain the lifelines of the islands. The amount of merchandise unloaded on the docks every week is staggering and continues to grow. One yardstick of this growth is the method of unloading. In the beginning, seamen handed cargo over the ship's side into whale boats, rowed the boats to shore, pulled them up on the beach and unloaded them by hand. Today cargo arrives in great metal boxes called containers, each with an average maximum content of 1,415 cubic square feet. They are stacked in the holds and on the decks of container ships like building blocks, each big enough to become a full load for a semitrailer truck on arrival. Monumental gantry cranes like giant robots lift the containers out of the ships and stack them on shore.

There is no exact information about how big a stack they would make if the containers were not immediately hauled away to feed, clothe and furnish the islands, but the estimates are mind boggling. Matson Navigation Co. makes three voyages to Hawaii in seven days, unloading 2,500 containers every week. This represents 70 to 75 per cent of the cargo landed from the West Coast of the United States but less than 50 per cent of all cargo. And it does not include autos unloaded in Hawaii nor the petroleum we consume.

Every week, ships bring 1,500 new cars to Hawaii, more than enough to fill the mall level parking lot at Ala Moana Center, the largest shopping complex in Honolulu. Every week, ships pump ashore 4,836,312 cubic feet (861,384 barrels) of oil, enough to fill twenty-eight stories of a high rise office building if it were constructed like a storage tank. The containers of merchandise would probably fill two more high rise office buildings of about the same height. It is no wonder that waterfront strikes in 1936 and in 1949 temporarily crippled the economy of Hawaii and caused bankruptcies of many small businesses dependent on ships for the goods they sold.

As opposed to this conveyor belt of cargo that bridges the ocean and attaches Hawaii firmly to the continent, more modest ocean activities are in progress that reinforce Hawaii's island identity in modern ways.

Surfing has exploded to a world wide popularity that even the most competitive of the old chiefs would have never predicted. And Hawaii remains the capital.

The resurgence of amateur outrigger canoe racing as a team ocean sport is almost as dramatic. Race officials said there were half a dozen canoe clubs on the island of Oahu twenty years ago. Today there are thirty-one canoe clubs on Oahu with an additional twenty-six on the neighbor islands and twelve more in the high schools. They compete in seven regattas during the year plus eight to ten long distance races. The premier event is the annual Molokai to Oahu Canoe Race over 40.8 miles of open ocean. More than fifty teams from around the world now compete.

Other uses of the ocean are increasing. Slips for yachts at the Ala Wai Yacht Harbor are in such demand that the waiting list is sometimes five years long. The boisterous reception for Trans Pacific Yacht Race crews who sail from California every two years has become the last vestige of boat day. The annual Hawaii International Billfish Tournament at Kailua, Kona has grown into a world famous event.

More than a million tourists every year sail on dinner cruises off Waikiki and on tours to Pearl Harbor. Cruise boats have become major users of our harbors. Leaders from the world of private finance, as well as government, support the new Hawaii Maritime Center, a museum of our ocean heritage, and plans for redevelopment of Honolulu Harbor.

Increased use of the ocean has caused new problems that also sensitize us to its importance in our lives. Spills caused by oil tankers generate newspaper headlines and public criticism. Marine debris, especially plastics, and gill net fishing have taken such a heavy toll of life in the ocean that restrictions reminiscent of old Hawaiian *kapus* are already in place.

A law against the use of drift gill nets in Hawaii waters has been passed in the State Legislature. The Marine Plastic Pollution Research and Control Act was passed in 1987 by the U.S. Congress in response to an international convention. The act prohibits dumping of plastics at sea and requires ports to have adequate waste collection facilities.

In both positive and negative terms, modern people of the islands and the world at large seem to be bonded to the ocean as firmly as the people of old.

Pupukea Area, North Shore, Oahu

Koko Head, Oahu

Nanakuli Beach Park, Oahu

Pupukea, Oahu

Leeward Side, Oahu

Kipahulu, Maui

Kaaawa Beach, Oahu

Waikiki Beach, Honolulu

Cave diving, Kona Coast, Hawaii

Canoe landing, South Kona, Hawaii

Felix's home and dog, Kona Coast, Hawaii

Charter boat, Kona, Hawaii

Man with fish trap

Bamboo Reef, Oahu

Felix, Kona, Hawaii

Eugene Kaupiko, "mayor" of Milolii, telling how the turtles swim

Offshore storm, Napoopoo, South Kona, Big Island

Squid catch, Waimanalo Beach Park, Oahu

Makapuu Point, Oahu

Makapuu, Oahu

Mokolii Island (Chinaman's Hat), Oahu

Rock divers, Waimea Bay, Oahu

Approved form for divers at "The Wall," Waikiki Beach

Kuhio Beach, Waikiki

"The Wall," Kuhio Beach

The Land

A newspaperman in Hawaii decided about twenty-five years ago to do some basic research. He stood on a Honolulu street corner and asked passersby, "Is there a limit to land?" The answers came without hesitation, "Of course, there is a limit to land. It stops at the shore." The same enterprising researcher asked the same question a short time later on a visit to Los Angeles. This time the responses were puzzled stares or laughter. To good natured Los Angelenos the question was like asking, "Can you walk to Chicago?" Of course, you can, but what's the point?

The point is that, when the supply of land is limited as on an island, and people accept the limitation as real, the first thing that happens is the price of that land goes up. The last twenty years of growth in the Los Angeles area have sent real estate prices soaring, an excellent indication that certain island adaptations are taking place there.

In the islands the upward spiral in real estate prices began earlier because the land is more limited. During the twenty-five years between 1950 and 1975, the price of land for tax appraisal purposes increased twenty-two times in the exclusive Waialae-Kahala residential section. The cost of land in Waikiki other than beach frontage increased seventeen times over the same period. Real estate prices in the rural valley of Makaha increased fifty-one times. In the upper middle class suburb of Aina Haina, a moderately priced three-bedroom house that cost $31,500 in 1959 has increased in price today, approximately three decades later, to $850,000. Homes in exclusive Kahala now sell in the tens of millions of dollars.

It may seem ironic that one lesson of islands, so long pictured as places where one can live cheaply under a coconut tree, is a high value placed on the land. Yet it has always been so. Disputes between chiefs in old Hawaii over who should control the largest land area provided endless excuses to wage war. Unless commoners made the land produce for a chief, they could expect to be dispossessed in favor of more desirable tenants.

But there was a major difference in the concept of ownership then compared to now. The land belonged to the gods. It could not be *owned* any more than the ocean or the sky could be *owned*. Chiefs, as descendants of the gods, merely held the land in trust for the gods, organizing its use and parceling it out for productive exploitation.

This concept of land as a gift of the gods gave rise to another attitude toward the land which is expressed in the term, *kamaaina*. *Kama* means child and *aina* means land. Thus, a *kamaaina* is a child of the land. In practical terms a *kamaaina* is an old timer, one who has always lived in a particular place as his ancestors had before him. But the meaning goes deeper. A *kamaaina* is a person who takes responsibility for the land he holds in trust for the gods, a person who cares for the land, who places upon it a high value and passes it on to be cared for by future generations. A *malihini* is a newcomer who takes no responsibility for the land. Consequently, his opinions carry little weight.

Another way in which old Hawaiians expressed the high value they placed upon the *aina* survives in poetic legend and the hula. Favorite themes are special places that stir the memory; mountain peaks tinted by cloud shadows, tropical valleys sleeping in the sun, ancestral homes, the beauty of waterfalls, places where certain flowers grow.

The closeness that the people of old felt to the *aina* is also reflected in Hawaiian names for the land. There was a name for every hill, every cliff, every cove, every beach, every cave. No feature of the landscape went without a name and each name was pregnant with meaning and history. The *kamaaina* of a particular valley understood these meanings and recited their history to the children so that they, too, might properly care for the land and preserve its traditions. In this way people became children of the land, attached to a particular place, known by that association.

The concept of land ownership by the gods proved unworkable for foreign businessmen who demanded firm titles. Missionaries also became impatient with the old system under which chiefs sometimes took selfish advantage of the common people. By western standards the old system of tenant farming discouraged enterprise. So the New England missionaries recommended to King Kamehameha III a system of fee simple or private land ownership that would release common people from servitude and motivate them to work for their own interests instead of the chiefs'. Each holder of a traditional plot of land or *kuleana* would become its owner and, like New England farmers on their small farms, would become a student of free enterprise.

Under a plan called the *Mahele* and put into effect in the late 1840s, the king was to receive one-third of the land to support the government. Another third would be portioned out to the chiefs, and the remaining third would be divided among commoners. King Kamehameha III approved the plan as a boon to his people, but it proved to be a disaster for them.

For the average Hawaiian, the papers he was expected to obtain for title to his *kuleana* were far more bewildering than the Form 1040 is to most taxpayers today. Most did not apply at all and lost their traditional holdings. A little more than 60 per cent of the land went to the government for its support and to the king for support of the royal household. Nearly 40 per cent went to the chiefs. But only .9 (nine-tenths of one) per cent of the land found its way into the hands of commoners and, of those, only 25 per cent received any land at all.

Those who profited most were foreigners who understood the new system. Chiefs immediately began selling land to cash in on their windfall. Commoners frequently lost land because they forgot they were supposed to now pay taxes on their *kuleanas*. Or they sold the land with little understanding of its value, then were forced to move. The *Great Mahele* in practical terms disenfranchised the Hawaiian people because they eventually lost control of the land. It was a change as fundamental as the overthrow of the old gods.

At the same time, the *Mahele* stimulated free enterprise. It made possible the accumulation of acreages for sugar plantations that provided, at last, an engine for the economy. Hawaii's prosperity and entree to the modern world is rooted in the *Great Mahele*. Changes of bewildering complexity grew out of the new land system and there is no better example of this than Waikiki.

Picture an inviting beach on the fringe of an extensive swamp. This is what the first Hawaiians found when they arrived at the place now advertised as the tourist capital of the Pacific. Streams from Manoa and Palolo Valleys debauched on the flat plain behind Waikiki Beach, creating a wilderness of marsh. The chief must have recognized the potential of the place at once. There was fishing on the reef and the waves curled just right for surfing. On this leeward coast the weather was almost always warm and dry but the streams provided fresh water to drink.

The greatest potential for food to feed the large population the chief intended his descendants to rule lay in the marsh. Flightless birds and other exotic game that fed there were soon hunted to extinction. But the swamp with its supply of fresh water could be transformed into taro patches. And so development of Waikiki began. The people built dykes and miles of irrigation ditches with a gentle fall that led the water placidly from taro patch to taro patch; miles of taro patches, a sea of taro patches.

Here was the true source of chiefly power, the reason for Waikiki's greatness, the reason it was the home of chiefs. And there was more. The people constructed fish ponds among the taro patches where the favorite fishes of the chiefs could be caught when the royal fancy dictated. Sugar cane grew along the dykes where people traveled. There grew also *wauke*, the mulberry plant whose bark produced *tapa*, and sweet potatoes. It was a development that displayed industry and ingenuity and engineering skills that combined the principles of farming, aquaculture and flood control. So Archibald Menzies, naturalist for Captain George Vancouver, found it teeming with people in 1792. He described the development of Waikiki with admiration.

Two years later another sea captain discovered the lagoon that became Honolulu Harbor, the only safe haven for deep water vessels in Hawaii at the time. The trading village that blossomed there drew the chiefs from Waikiki and, with them, the people. Foreign diseases decimated the population. Taro no longer represented the wealth of the land. The patches fell into disuse and, with the arrival of the mosquito in 1826, became breeding grounds for aggravation.

Foreigners discovered the charms of Waikiki Beach and built summer houses there, especially after engineers in the 1880s finally figured out how to pipe in fresh water that could come out of a tap. A modest real estate boom resulted. Mansions went up and eventually became hotels. By that time the taro patches, the glory of old Waikiki, had been converted to rice paddies or were reverting to swamp. In the 1920s they were drained by the Ala Wai Canal. Coral fill provided a firm foundation for new development.

Where taro once grew now sprout luxury hotels and high rise condominiums. Waikiki again has become a producer of incredible wealth, a resort for the chiefs of the world. Land that once belonged to the gods is now worth many hundreds of dollars per square foot on the real estate market. There are few places in the world where land costs so much. But few residents of Hawaii can afford to own it. Much of it belongs to or is controlled by people from somewhere else.

Kamaaina of all races feel a vague sense of dispossession. The cost of land in the islands is a major challenge to the survival of special values that make us human and give us our identity. Hawaiians have long struggled with the problem and now we all are.

Volcanoes National Park, Hawaii

Near Hana, Maui

North Kona, Hawaii

Waianae Coast, Oahu

Nuuanu Valley, Oahu

North Oahu

Makena, Maui

Kula, Maui

Iao Valley, Maui

Kipahulu, Maui

Road near Haena, Kauai

Cane road, West Maui Mountains

Kipahulu, Maui

Kipahulu, Maui

Haleiwa, Oahu

Hanalei, Kauai

Cemetery, Kipahulu, Maui

Lanai Island from Lahaina, Maui

Puuhonua o Honaunau, Hawaii

Who Are We?

"**I**t has become harder and harder to define people," said Robert C. Schmitt, statistician who compiles the annual State of Hawaii Data Book that provides information about the highest, hottest, wettest, noisiest and most heavily populated places in the islands. Every year Schmitt digs up new and more intriguing statistics about Hawaii and its multiethnic people. And every year he becomes more confused about who we are.

When Hawaii became a State of the Union in 1959, about one-third of the babies born to island residents were racially mixed. By 1979, the percentage of ethnically mixed babies overtook that of unmixed babies. The percentage of mixed babies is still rising. In 1988, 55.8 per cent of the babies born to island residents faced the new world with two or more racial or ethnic backgrounds. Schmitt admits that this confusion has reduced race-related census figures in Hawaii to statistical chaos.

Definitions of race have become so fuzzy, he said, that census takers now classify people according to local usage if they prefer. This leads to additional complications. If you happen to be Hawaiian-Chinese-Portugese-Irish, you could be listed as any of the above:

One—If the census taker asks what race you are and you say, "Irish," that is the race you become.

Two—If you answer that you are racially mixed and ask him, "What does that make me?" the census taker will put down the race of your mother which could make you Portuguese. However, if the census had been taken fifteen years ago, the rule at that time required the census taker to put down the race of your father which could have made you Chinese.

Three—If you receive the census questionnaire in the mail, you will be classified by the first race you put down. That would make you Hawaiian.

Schmitt himself is married to a lady who is one of fifteen children born to Chinese-Hawaiian parents. Nearly all of the fifteen children married people of different racial backgrounds including Filipino, Korean, Caucasian and Japanese. Curious, statistician Schmitt asked them how they answered the census takers. One of his in-laws confessed that he answered, "Chinese," because he felt the census taker was asking for his favorite racial strain in the family. Another in-law said she answered, "Well, my name is Japanese now." Schmitt said, "They were all trying to figure out what the census taker wanted. But they really consider themselves racially mixed."

Such cultural diversity has turned Hawaii into a place of provocative images that constantly pose questions; "What's going on here, who are we?"

Slippers on the lanai can belong to half a dozen different races. Hawaiian *heiau* or Buddhist temples sprout amid freeways or downtown traffic. Supermarkets carry the ingredients for Chinese, Japanese, Korean, Filipino, Hawaiian feasts as well as pizza, bagels,

French bread and sauerkraut. The faces of cheer leaders at football games offer complex studies in ethnic background.

All of this can lead to acute identity problems that are probably the most difficult for Hawaiians who started it all. For better or worse, Hawaiian women made little distinction between the races of foreigners who came to their shores in increasing numbers, and, their lives were uncomplicated with restrictions about sex. From the beginning, babies of mixed race began to appear. By the 1840s, concern surfaced for the welfare of beautiful *hapa haole*, half-foreign girls born to Hawaiian women and primarily Caucasian men. A cantankerous old merchant established a school to teach the girls sewing and letters so that they might shine in polite society. It was the first public recognition of this identity problem. Acceptance of mixed parentage grew as the number of babies increased. By the 1880s, *hapa haoles* had became important figures in business, government and society.

But who were they, Hawaiian or Caucasian? The problem came into sharp focus during the revolution of 1893 in which Caucasian annexationists overthrew the Hawaiian monarchy. Where did one's loyalty lie? Almost the entire Royal Hawaiian Band quit in protest against taking an oath of allegiance to the new haole Provisional Government. Another *hapa haole* government worker said he was willing to take the oath to keep his job but his wife would divorce him if he did.

The conflict between one's Hawaiian heritage and one's Caucasian background cuts all sorts of ways. For many years, churches looked upon the hula as sinful and Kamehameha Schools expelled *hapa haole* students for doing the dance on campus. In a *hula halau* students were taught reverence for the beauties of nature, to feel as a loving family, and how to express the artistic soul of the race. The *haole* side emphasized competition. The Hawaiian side emphasized cooperation. *Haole* children raised their hands in class to show how much they had learned. To Hawaiian children, such pushing oneself forward was rude.

Yet, while the pure Hawaiian race decreased in numbers, the numbers of part-Hawaiians grew. In 1900, full blooded Hawaiians made up 19 per cent of the total population, part-Hawaiians only 6 per cent. By 1950, the percentage of full blooded

Hawaiians had decreased to 3 per cent while the percentage of part-Hawaiians had increased to 16 per cent. Today, less than 1 per cent of the population is pure Hawaiian but part-Hawaiians comprise about 20 per cent. Part-Hawaiians now make up the third largest racial group in the islands exceeded only by Caucasians and Japanese.

While the purity of the race waned, more and more of its attractive culture entered the mainstream. How extensively this has happened is best shown by an example. Part-Hawaiian public school students at Waianae on Oahu in 1970 traveled to the Navajo Reservation in Arizona for an exchange with students there. A journalist from Honolulu accompanied the students and their teachers. On the reservation the newspaperman became acquainted with Navajo teachers. He learned that the Navajo women, unlike Hawaiians, seldom marry outside of their race.

An anthropologist from Arizona State College in nearby Flagstaff visited the reservation for a program of Hawaiian and Indian dances. The journalist from Hawaii asked him how many Navajo words were in common usage in Flagstaff. The anthropologist thought for a minute and answered that the only word that might qualify would be "hogan" or house. How many classes were there in Flagstaff where people could learn Navajo dances? None. How many Flagstaff restaurants served Navajo foods? None. How many juke boxes played Navajo songs? None. How many shops featured clothing inspired by Navajo styles? None. In the islands, Hawaiian words, foods, dances, songs and styles are everywhere.

One reason for this is that the charm and attractiveness of Hawaiian culture is a basic ingredient of the tourist industry. The hula and songs of the islands are staples of entertainment in Waikiki. Old legends about prominent landmarks add enjoyment to guided tours. The radio program, "Hawaii Calls," for years provided tropical escape for snowbound listeners on the mainland.

Yet the very popularity of things Hawaii may intensify the Hawaiian identity problem rather than ease it. The growth of tourism has coincided with criticism from some people who consider themselves Hawaiian that not only the land, but the culture is being taken from them. There is also concern that native Hawaiians have not received their proper share of the profits from tourism.

Such feelings have contributed to a new militancy among Hawaiians and to a cultural rebirth called the Hawaiian Renaissance. Beginning in a protest over evictions of tenants from farm land, the movement blossomed into pride of identity. A whole new generation of young Hawaiian song writers have introduced exciting new sounds. A renewed interest in the ancient hula, *kahiko,* has spread to all the islands. Today the annual hula competition in Hilo, The Merry Monarch Festival, is one of the outstanding cultural events of the Pacific. It is performed by and for Hawaiians.

The year 1976 saw the first voyage of the double-hulled *Hokule'a,* a 60-foot-long replica of an ancient Polyensian voyaging canoe. She sailed to Tahiti with a Hawaiian crew on the path of early migrations to Hawaii. Her navigator steered by the stars and the set of the waves without benefit of compass or sextant. In 1985 *Hokule'a* set out on a two-year, 12,000-mile Voyage of Rediscovery that retraced every major Polynesian migration route in the Pacific. She touched Tahiti, the Cook Islands, New Zealand, Tonga, Samoa and the Tuamotus. By this time the crew of *Hokule'a* have become veteran voyagers in the heroic tradition of their ancestors and the canoe itself has become one of Hawaii's historic vessels.

A similar resurgence of cultural identity is stirring among other races in Hawaii. Koreans have built a new cultural center. Japanese in 1985 celebrated the centennial of large scale immigration to Hawaii. Chinese in 1989 celebrated their bicentennial in the islands. The art festivals, dance programs, banquets and parties that make up these celebrations permit everybody to join in. More and more families of all races are tracing their genealogies and visiting their ancestral villages. It is as if the threat of homogenization has awakened a need to assert individuality.

All of this results in a delightfully complex society that residents value for its cultural complexity and then continue to intermarry, making it still more complex. There is a haunting similarity between this proliferation of identities on small islands and the startling number of species evolved by land snails, fruit flies and other nonhuman immigrants long ago. It is a phenomenon that seems to be occuring globally as small nations and ethnic groups within nations assert their identities. A shrinking of our world seems to accentuate the value of everybody being different.

So Hawaii cannot be called a melting pot. People are proud of being "mixed," not homogenized. The term they use to describe this racial mixture is "local," a word that carries connotations of *kamaaina* but is more militant and emphasizes the difference between residents of Hawaii and people anywhere else. The way to become a part of this cultural grab bag is to enjoy it, not to claim blood brotherhood or sisterhood but to respect the differences that exist, and to give them room to breathe.

The results can be startling. Within walking distance of the downtown Honolulu financial district are Chinese herb stores, MacDonald's hamburger havens, Japanese noodle factories, art galleries, flower lei stands, shops selling Vietnamese wedding costumes and an open air fish market. End-of-the-day workers heading out on King Street have an unlimited choice of fast foods to take home; chop suey, pizza, sushi, Kentucky Fried Chicken, Korean barbecue, tacos, sweet sour spare ribs, Hawaiian plate and many more.

Nowhere does Hawaii's ethnic complexity bloom in such exotic splendor as on opening day of the State Legislature when politicians provide a free lunch for their supporters. One office will serve Filipino chicken feet while voters next door are eating chocolate chip cookies. Some politicians specialize in produce of their districts; Kona coffee, Maui onions. Others specialize in fish; dried, boiled, baked, fried in the tradition of a dozen different cultures. From tuna salad to Chinese noodles, the legislative free lunch is a showcase of the cultural diversity in Hawaii.

So it seems only fitting that Governor John Waihee, part-Hawaiian, once compared racial mixing in the islands not to a milk shake but to Hawaiian stew. He is a student of Hawaiian stew because he grew up in the Waimea ranch land on the Big Island of Hawaii where the cowboys ate stew five times a week. It might taste differently each time depending on who made it; a German-Hawaiian father, and Irish-Hawaiian mother, a Chinese-Hawaiian grandmother or whomever. From this boyhood experience, Waihee insists that he can name the ethnic background of a stew chef just by tasting because each of us adds a different ingredient, an herb, or a spice, that gives the bowl its distinctive flavor.

Waipio Valley, Hawaii

Cane Road, West Maui

The Road at Kipahulu, Maui

Near Lahaina, Maui

Kaneohe Bay, Oahu

Puuhonua o Honaunau, Hawaii

Puuhonua o Honaunau, Hawaii

Poamoho Camp, Oahu

Hauula, Oahu

Milolii, Hawaii

Kapiolani Park, Honolulu

104

Kuhio Beach breakwater, Waikiki

An ohana

Kakaako, Honolulu

Zori montage, Kawela, Oahu

Kalakaua Avenue, Waikiki

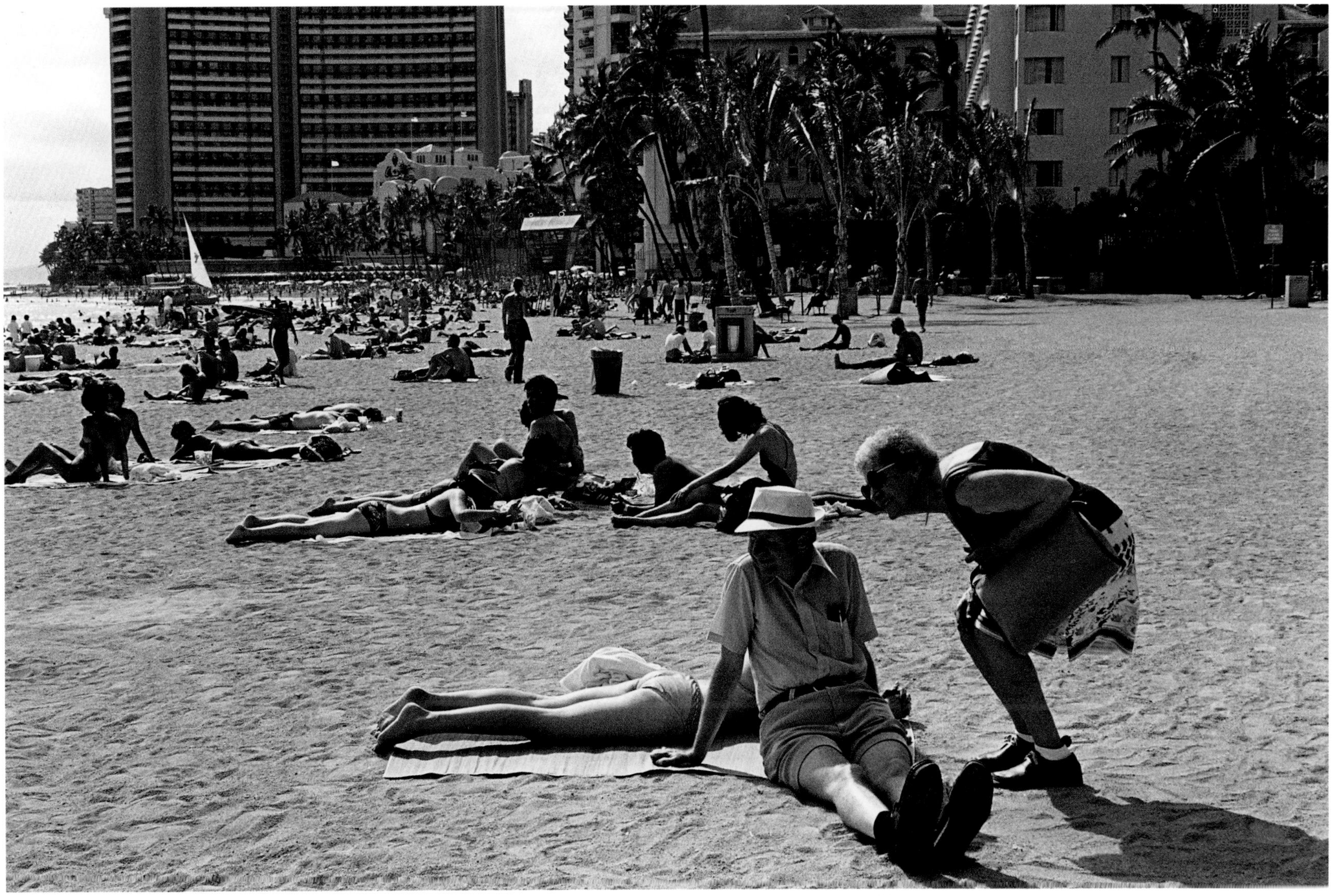

Waikiki Beach, Honolulu

Ranches on Maui and Hawaii

Cattle ranch on the slopes of Haleakala, Maui

Kapiolani Park, Waikiki

Kaahumanu Society at Iolani Palace, Honolulu

Holualoa, Hawaii

Haleiwa, Oahu

Barbershop, Hanapepe, Kauai

116

Honolulu Memorial at Punchbowl National Cemetery

Honolulu Academy of Arts

Memories of North Kona, Hawaii

The Wo Hing Temple, Lahaina, Maui

Near Makapala, Hawaii

Church, Molokai

The Ishizuchi Shrine on South King Street, Honolulu

College Walk, Honolulu, sculpture by Edward M. Brownlee

Wo On Store, Halawa, North Kohala, Hawaii

University of Hawaii, the Bilger Hall with a mural by David Asherman

Waikiki Beach, Honolulu

Puuhonua o Honaunau, Hawaii

Pacific Herb Shop, North King Street, Honolulu

Punahou School Carnival, Honolulu

The Old Pali Road, Oahu

Old Gods and New Technology

The leading causes of change in Hawaii during the past two hundred years have been the technologies that enrich our lives and, at the same time, tend to dehumanize us. There is no better example of this than the Honolulu International Airport. This gateway to high adventure has grown from a shed beside a coral-topped landing field to become the largest, most confusing building complex in the islands and it continues to change like a never completed construction project.

These changes follow each other so rapidly that Honolulu's most indispensable public servant may be Warland Kealoha whose technology consists of making the signs that direct traffic around the changes. He is sometimes a week behind making signs that keep the 11½ million people a year who arrive and depart the airport from losing their way to the bathroom. He estimates that it takes about 25 signs just to direct passengers from taxis outside the terminal through the maze of corridors into a jet liner bound for Tokyo. And each time somebody digs up a sidewalk or adds a new boarding gate, the signs change.

Disorientation caused by airport technology is minor compared to the daily frustration inflicted by our automobiles. Since the first horseless carriage arrived in Hawaii in 1899, road builders have been trying to keep up with the need for streets and highways. But they never catch up. By the last count, there were 628,000 licensed drivers in the state, and 4,071 miles of roadway. This works out to 154 drivers for every mile of roadway or 34 feet of street or highway for every driver.

Fortunately, not everybody drives at the same time. But every once in a while enough drivers get the urge simultaneously and the result is grid lock. Such a calamity took place early in January of 1989 when Chinese celebrated the bicentennial of their arrival in the islands with a big fireworks display at Ala Moana Park. The $1 million extravaganza began at 8:30 p.m. An hour before the first rocket went off, streets for a mile in all directions were bumper to bumper automobiles. Some 11,000 cars jammed into the nearby parking lot of the Ala Moana Shopping center which was designed for 7,800. It was midnight before everybody got home.

The headaches of morning and evening rush hour in Honolulu is daily lunch hour conversation. Like the weather, everybody talks about traffic but nobody seems able to do much about it. Government officials have been arguing for twenty years about fixed rail mass transit. Every attempt to provide alternative transportation by water taxi has failed for lack of passengers. Bicycle riders deserve medals for heroism on streets dominated by the rest of us who insist on driving cars.

Because the automobile, like so many technological marvels, is a source of pleasure as well as frustration. Our cars give us status and pride of ownership, freedom to go when and where we please. Though we may exert less control over our lives than did our ancestors, the horsepower under the hood gives us a sense of power. The Yellow Pages of the

Honolulu phone book, that accurate barometer of social evolution, lists by far more pages for the welfare of our automobiles than for any other aspect of our lives including our health and the salvation of our souls. We are willing to give up a great deal for our automobiles because they remove some of our limitations and make us bigger than ourselves.

So it should come as no surprise that new technologies which erased old limitations proved attractive to island people upon the arrival of European explorers. Hawaiians placed the highest value at first on iron because it freed them from the drudgery of making stone tools that blunted quickly and broke more easily than metal. Longer acquaintance with Western technology transferred the choice for most wanted trade goods to muskets and cannons that provided ambitious chiefs with more fire power. The battle that sealed the overthrow of the old gods was won by muskets. Hawaiian women preferred cloth, a vast improvement over *tapa* because it did not tear so easily and could be washed.

Not all Hawaiians approved of the popular craving for the products of new technologies. Kamehameha, last of the great war chiefs and conqueror of all the islands, owned uniforms and dress suits but he preferred to wear the *malo* or loincloth. When traders discovered sandalwood in the islands and offered enticing merchandise for it, Kamehameha placed a *kapu* on sandalwood trees to preserve some of the wealth for future generations. Kamehameha never forgot the limitations of the islands, a concept out of which the old gods evolved. When horses arrived in Hawaii in 1803, he refused one as a gift because it would eat too much.

The old chief defended the gods until he died in 1819. But by that time the limitations he and the gods recognized had already been overrun. Young men sailed away in foreign ships beyond the reach of the gods and returned with undreamed of luxuries like stylish caps and bell bottom trousers. Kamehameha took these things away from them. He sternly enforced the old *kapus* that relegated women to second class status. Yet his favorite wife, Kaahumanu, broke the *kapus* behind his back and ate foods not allowed women. When Kamehameha died, it was Kaahumanu who led the overthrow of the gods.

Residents of the islands have been embracing and shaping their economy around new technologies ever since. The sandalwood trade lapsed as the leading business activity in

Hawaii because the chiefs, contrary to Kamehameha's advice, exhausted the supply of sandalwood. Whaling rose as the economic mainstay with the discovery of rich breeding grounds in the North Pacific. Many of Honolulu's most prestigious firms made their first profits as suppliers to whale ships and by shipping the oil to eastern markets. The insatiable demand for whale oil eventually exhausted the supply of whales.

It was about the time of the U.S. Civil War that pioneer planters began investing energy and money in sugar cane, a crop that grew uncommonly well in Hawaii and for which there was a world wide market. From the beginning, buyers recognized Hawaiian sugar for its superior quality. A treaty of reciprocity with the United States in 1876 removed the tariff on Hawaiian sugar sold in the U.S. and turned a growing industry into a incredibly profitable one. For the next twenty years, sugar plantations in the islands multiplied like mushrooms. The industry created a new demand for land and also for cheap labor. Importation of workers from all over the world, but primarily Asia, fundamentally changed the complexion of Hawaii's population.

Unlike sandalwood and whaling, the land that produced sugar was a renewable resource. Criticism of the industry aimed less at its exploitation of limited resources than at the division of the profits and a monopoly of the land by sugar factors who controlled Hawaii's economy for half a century. The leading companies were called the Big Five. All had their origins in sugar plantations and shipping, and gradually expanded into finance, retailing and other activities including philanthrophy.

Paternalistic control by the Big Five gave way after World War II upset the established order. Strikes by sugar workers that had been minor irritants before the war became major upheavals when workers joined the union. Planters responded to rising labor costs by mechanizing. Superior sugar technology kept the growers in business.

Tourism remained a charming but backward child who refused to grow up until the jet airplane and statehood in 1959 made a tourist bureau slogan come true: "Hawaii, closer than you think. Lovelier than you dream." The 1960s ushered in an economic boom generated by tourism that created new fortunes and soon established the visitor industry as Hawaii's number one economic force.

The economic boom that followed Statehood projected Hawaii firmly into the jet age, the world of computers and the era of satellite communication. When that boom began, the Honolulu Symphony played in McKinley High School auditorium to an audience in hard, wooden seats. Today the symphony plays in a stylish, air conditioned concert hall. When the boom began, the home of sports in Hawaii was a cramped and rickety wooden structure known as "Termite Palace." Today television cameras beam bowl games around the nation from comfortable and commodious Aloha Stadium. A common complaint before the boom began was a lack of something to do. Today the weekly "TGIF (Thank God It's Friday)" section of *The Honolulu Advertiser* lists pages of activities for the coming week.

In spite of a nostalgic longing for the good old days, there is little indication that anybody is willing to trade automatic washers, kitchen appliances and air conditioning for the drudgery and inconvenience of washboards, coal stoves and kerosene lanterns. Yet, there is growing concern that we are buying these conveniences at the price of energy resources that cannot be replaced at the rate we are consuming them. The best estimates for the life span of our fossil fuel civilization is that it will last perhaps another 150 years at present projections of energy consumption.

For Hawaii and for people everywhere, all of this could mean a bleak future or it could open the most exciting era in history. Like the old Hawaiians, we are bathed in perpetual energy from the sun. There is inexhaustible energy in the waves and the wind. Energy sprouts out of the ground as trees and other plants. It erupts from the craters of volcanoes. The cost of collecting this renewable energy and putting it to use in the amounts we need to maintain our living standard is, in most cases, far higher at present than the cost of fossil fuel energy. This is the technological challenge.

Hawaii, uncomplicated by nuclear power plants, is a natural laboratory for experimentation because more than 90 per cent of the energy produced in the islands today comes from imported petroleum. Technologies to harness renewable energy have been seriously pursued only in the last twenty years or so but are already making headlines.

Ronald Hayes, president and chief executive officer of the Pacific International

Center for High Technology Research, and his staff have pointed out that the island of Kauai today generates 37 per cent of its electricity from renewable sources including hydroelectric power. Thirty-four per cent of the electricity generated on the island of Hawaii comes from renewable sources including volcano heat, and by bagasse, the refuse of cane stalks from which the juice has been squeezed out and which can be burned as fuel. Molokai generates 40 percent of its electricity, and Maui 20 percent. It is estimated that on Oahu, the heaviest user of energy, wind generators can eventually supply 40 per cent of electricity consumption.

The most elegant new technology is called Ocean Thermal Energy Conversion (OTEC). After successful experiments, a pilot plant is planned for the Kona Coast of Hawaii where ocean water is used to produce clean energy. Warm surface water produces steam in a vacuum and the steam generates electricity. Cold water from the ocean depths condenses the steam and produces fresh water while operating an air conditioning unit. Such a unit reduced the electricity bill of the experimental laboratory by $400 a month.

By-products of this technology are equally useful. The fresh water, rich in nutrients, flows into tanks where fish grow much faster than normally. A new aquaculture industry is springing out of OTEC research. From the tanks the nutrient rich water flows into the ocean where, it is hoped, it will create new breeding grounds for fish and, thus, increase the food supply. Hayes said one OTEC plant has the potential of lighting 1,000 homes in addition to its other benefits.

None of these technological marvels will provide an easy, simple and painless substitute for fossil fuels. But the technology can reduce the pain of withdrawal and provide time to find new technologies. Dr. John Bardach, senior advisor to the president of the East-West Center, gave examples of how much difference energy efficient technologies available today can make tomorrow; from a saving of 81 per cent by using state of the art light bulbs to 50 per cent by driving cars that go 70 miles on a gallon of gas.

Yet this is not the most exciting aspect of the changes we face. It is the opportunity to learn new skills, to experience new relationships with people, to try on new attitudes for size, to expand our potential as human beings.

Kapiolani Park and Waikiki, Oahu

Kamuela, Hawaii

Hanalei Valley, Kauai

Kaneohe Bay, Oahu

Pineapple fields, Oahu

Puhi Post Office, Kauai

Haleiwa Strained Poi, taro dock

Nuuanu Avenue, downtown Honolulu

Sidewalk enterprise, Beretania Street

Store, Haleiwa, Oahu

Sugar mill, Waialua, Oahu

Bas-relief by Tom van Sant, Davies Pacific Center, Honolulu

Net mending, Honolulu Harbor

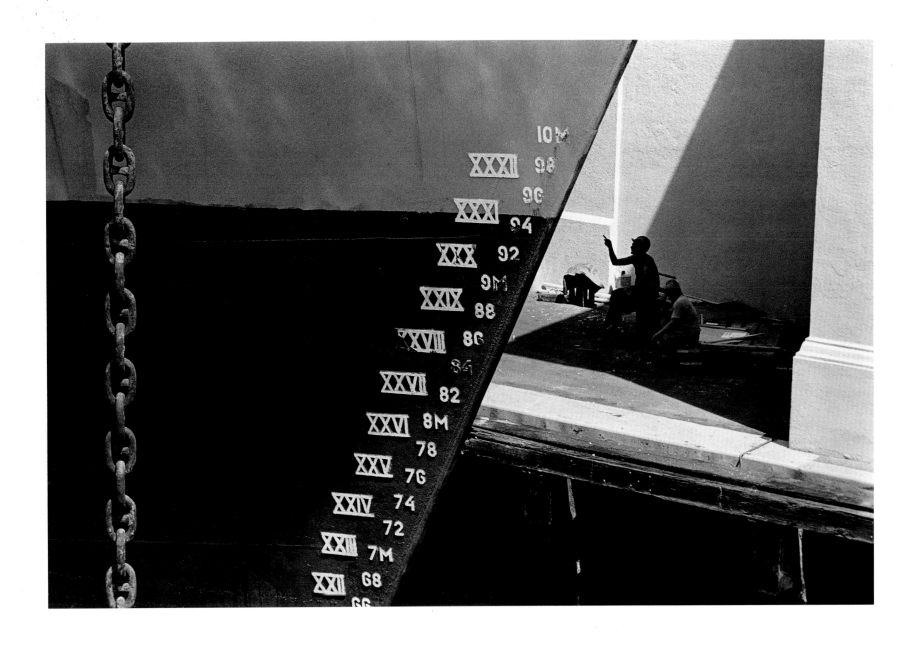

Pier 8, Honolulu Harbor

150

U.S.S. Arizona and Memorial, Pearl Harbor, Oahu

The Hawaii Maritime Center, Honolulu Harbor

Japanese fishing boat heading seaward, Honolulu Harbor

153

Young Brothers Barge, Honolulu Harbor

Waikiki Beach, Honolulu

Cocktails at the Moana Hotel, Waikiki Beach

Kamehameha's Statue at Aliiolani Hale, Honolulu

Father Damien Statue at the Hawaii State Capitol, Honolulu

158

Aloha Friday concert in Tamarind Park

Aloha Friday in Tamarind Park, downtown Honolulu

Bank of Hawaii, Honolulu

Kozo Sushi, Union Mall and King Street downtown, Honolulu

At the Hawaii State Capitol

Honolulu

Ala Moana Shopping Center, Saturday afternoon

Ala Moana Shopping Center, Honolulu

Hickam Air Force Base, Oahu

Pacific Resources Inc. Refinery, Barber's Point, Oahu

How We Cope

At least 4.5 million people every year choose Waikiki as a place of escape from the boredom of 9 A.M. to 5 P.M. jobs, the frustration of rush hour traffic jams or the pressure of crowded cities. These people expect to return home sun tanned (or burned) and relaxed. Enough of them do so to maintain the reputation of Waikiki as an exotic haven for the bored, the weary and those afflicted with nervous tension.

There is a paradox in this. The daytime population of Waikiki—when residents are at home, hotel workers have arrived from around the island, and tourists are on the beach or in the shops—adds up to 82,305 persons per square mile. Most of the tourists who visit Waikiki live in places with population densities considerably less crowded. To be honest, there are few places in the world with population densities as high as 82,305 per square mile. Yet visitors come to Waikiki to relax.

How can this be? By what magic, other than coconut palms and a sunny beach, are people able to cast away stress where sidewalks are thronged with people, restaurants are crowded with diners and the streets are jammed with traffic?

The secret, of course, is that these people are not in a hurry. They don't stride down Kalakaua Avenue, they stroll. They are not in competition. They have not come to be critical but to enjoy themselves and one another. They don't snarl at waitresses, they smile. In doing so, they provide space for themselves and everyone else. It is a classic method of coping with the small size of an island.

Hawaiians developed similar behavior as a survival technique but it is not behavior common among folks taught to conquer continents, break speed records and pave the world with freeways. For Napoleon Bonaparte, whose ambition girdled the globe, islands became prisons. Many U.S. soldiers and marines sent to the South Pacific during World War II referred to the tropical islands on which they were stationed as "The Rock." Quite a few new residents in Honolulu zoom around the island in one afternoon and then complain that there is nowhere else to go.

So the basic requirement for coping with the limitations of an island is a state of mind. We can chose, for example, between the achievement of driving around the islands faster than anybody else or the enjoyment of slowing down and studying the endless complexity of people and cultures and nature along the way. We must decide which person is better equipped to survive on a planet that is constantly shrinking in size, one who complains that we are overwhelmed with problems or another who finds the new dimension full of exciting potential?

The excitement in adjusting to the limitations of an island comes from developing skills we didn't know we had and finding value in what seemed less important before. Courtesy, for example. It is embarrassing to come face to face with someone to whom you have been rude the last time you met. On an island this happens all the time. It does not take long to learn that the survival value of courtesy on an island goes up while the value of self-importance goes down because we are so vulnerable to one another. It is often smarter to be polite than right, to grit your teeth and smile. More and more tourists have made this discovery in foreign countries.

A similar attitude extends to tolerance for different religions and races and customs. The Hawaiian name for such courtesy and tolerance is the *Aloha Spirit*. It is more an expression of survival than sentiment in a shrinking world where racial slurs can receive wide publication and create a dangerous backlash. In Hawaii, where every race is a minority, this situation has existed for a long time. The result of learning to get along together has been a discovery that this is a delightful way to live.

So Hawaii has taken as a title, the Aloha State. It is the only one named after an attitude. This complicated state of mind sometimes baffles new arrivals. One problem is learning to recognize important people because they don't dress the part. In Honolulu today the only executives who regularly wear suits and ties are attorneys and real estate salesmen. Attorneys have to wear coats in court but nobody has been able to figure out why real estate salesmen do it.

Shoes are also expendable. City Councilman Gary Gill once admitted that he didn't wear shoes until, as a teenager, he took a trip to Europe. By the time he got home his calluses were gone, and he's been wearing shoes ever since. Highly competent secretaries sit at desks with their shoes off while typing letters. It is common practice to take one's shoes off when entering a house. You can frequently tell the size of the family, or the number of visitors, by the collection of shoes on the doorstep.

More important adaptations are less noticeable. Business executives eventually discover that credibility on an island comes less from flaunting wealth or power than from how it is used to benefit the community. David Heenan, president and chief executive officer of Theo. H. Davies, Ltd., once put it this way: "There is a more holistic concept here. You could be the wealthiest person in Hawaii and still not be considered a leader." Robert Reed, president, chief executive officer and chairman of the board of Pacific Resources, Inc., said, "Money is a standard of success but executives are also measured by success in community affairs." A female executive commented, "At a beach picnic, it doesn't matter who has a million dollars."

This is why *kamaaina* millionaires in Hawaii are usually low key, soft spoken people who prefer not to make headlines while exercising power.

Most of the adaptations the old Hawaiians evolved for coping with their vulnerability to one another are simply techniques for enjoying each other. Privacy in old Hawaii was valued less than togetherness. It was so on other Pacific Islands. One of the first Peace Corpsmen on the island of Truk said he was taken into the home of a Micronesian family. They even permitted him to put up a cloth that shielded his bed because he was used to having his own room at home. Still the constant mingling with family members grated on his nerves. Visitors constantly came and went.

He said he learned the language and got used to the food but the lack of privacy drove him up the wall. One day he escaped during a party to the coconut grove where he sat on a stump just to be alone. His host left the party to sit beside him so he wouldn't be lonely.

Obviously, learning to live together in a crowded world could solve many problems today at little cost; traffic, for example. The overwhelming majority of cars in the longest traffic jams contain only one person. If we could learn to enjoy each other so much that driving alone would be lonely, traffic jams would disappear because one-half to three-quarters of our cars would stay in the garage. Or we might prefer the bus. For years in Tahiti, Le Truck, the jitney bus, was a favorite arena of social contact, the place to hear the latest news and to compare genealogies. If city buses performed the same service today they might attract more riders.

Other old adaptations have been passed down with minor modifications; the feast, for example. For the people of old, the feast provided a cooperative alternative to the competitiveness of war. The feast appealed not to the human fondness of excitement and danger but to the equally human fondness for pleasure, status and social contact.

There were ritual feasts on the *heiau* for the gods. There were feasts to bless a new house, to recognize important guests, to honor the first born, to celebrate the completion of a new irrigation ditch or taro patch. The importance of each feast lay not only in the gathering of great numbers of people in friendly contact but in the extensive cooperative effort required to make it all possible and in the conferring of status upon an approved project or person. At the same time, the feast distributed wealth and welded the bonds of the community.

Family "baby *luaus*" and church benefit *luaus* today are direct descendants of the old, traditional feast and they serve the same purpose. The feast also appears in many other modifications; school carnivals, cultural festivals, political fund raisers, honorary banquets. Christmas is our biggest modern feast. It honors the Christ Child, brings families and whole communities together in good fellowship, provides a cessation of competitive activity and an opportunity to feel good by sharing. Merchants have discovered that there is no stronger incentive for stimulating the economy and distributing wealth.

All this means that the tides of change may sweep us in directions we did not expect to go. What we find on our island may not be escape, but ourselves. It depends on our state of mind.

West Maui

Windsurfers at Diamond Head Beach, Oahu

Hanauma Bay, Oahu

Leeward Side, Oahu

Mokolii Island (Chinaman's Hat), Oahu

Kuhio Beach Park, Honolulu

Picnic at Queen's Beach, Honolulu

Keanae Point, Maui

Waikiki Beach

Zen archer, Kapiolani Park, Honolulu

Kapiolani Park, Waikiki

Hulihuli chicken sale, Oahu

Taste from the imu (underground oven)

Hula Hot Dogs, Honolulu

Aala Park, Honolulu

Young cheer leaders, Oahu

Young baseball players, Oahu

Softball, Oahu

Kapiolani Park, Honolulu

192

The bridge at King and River Streets, Honolulu

Acrobats, Honolulu

Island kids and their friend

Waikiki Beach, Honolulu

Body surfer at Diamond Head

Queen's Beach, Honolulu

MacFarlane Regatta, 4th of July, Waikiki

Cheetah, Transpac Race boat, after arrival in Honolulu

Artist on "The Wall," Waikiki

Sunrise at Waikiki Beach, Honolulu

About The Photography

It's difficult to realize that this photography spans more than a quarter century. When I came to the islands in 1959, I began a love affair that continues to this day. I plunged into a world of many cultures, set in a sublime natural environment, bathed by the most soothing climate in the world. I found an ease of living, a pleasure in life, everywhere I turned. I felt this was the world as it was meant to be.

As a photographer and artist, I began creating studies of the myriad subjects that seemed important. I set forth with my cameras in search of whatever inner truth this wondrous world might reveal to me. In this very personal pursuit, I was led from mountaintop to ocean floor, through every village on each island, over the beaches and cliffs and into the forests. I travelled light, trying to walk slowly and be as invisible as possible. The magic before my eyes was something fragile, and to best create an artistic impression of it I felt I dare not disturb the myriad worlds through which I moved.

My goal was to "capture" a fleeting spirit, the personality of the people and the islands. Through the years I've worked in various styles. Always my concern was to put an impression on film of a precariously delicate, yet beautiful way of life. I worked with urgency, fearing some unknown element might creep in to change this magical world I'd found. I rushed from one place to another, dizzied by new visions around every corner.

Because of the nature of my quest, most of my work is done with reflex cameras: Nikon or Hasselblad. Much was done with lenses slightly longer or shorter than "normal" focal length. My best work seems to come as a spontaneous reaction to some visual stimulus. With my left eye (which I almost lost in a car crash in Mexico) I seem instinctively able to frame and compose elements of a photograph through the lens in a single thought. I seldom debate or rearrange that which this visual instinct dictates through the lens. I've often thought this was laziness on my part, but the more I "intellectualize" an image, the more I return to the original impulse. Some of this results from the endless times I've lifted the camera to my eye, and learned what is seen by a particular lens. This spontaneous approach was necessary, since most of my images are but brief glimpses that vanish in a heartbeat. I'm just thankful to have been in the right place and that the shutter opened when it did.

This book is about change. It is also about human values, and an underlying spirit that seems eternal. Although the physical face of the islands is changing as we rush into the 21st century, I still find threaded throughout this growing and dynamic place that constant and undefinable spirit of aloha. Now that I work only part of the year in the islands I'm more aware how fast changes occur . . . and still more aware how unchanging is this magical underlying spirit. Working on the book this summer I saw new vitality and energy everywhere: new buildings, stores, businesses. Yet, everywhere I found the same gracious and warm human values that give meaning to the word "aloha." I feel this joy of life is as visible in the photograph I made last month of three girls on King Street as it was in images done twenty years ago.

I feel this book is an important statement about what Hawaii is, was, and will be. To me it's not just a series of photographs of "another pretty place." Rather, it's an impression, an artistic interpretation of an evolving way of life and the underlying values that make Hawaii one of the most wonderful places on earth . . .

Rick Golt
Sweden, Maine

I want to extend warmest thanks to my wife, Piggy, who believed in the dream; to my son Damien, who taught me the patience to persist; to Andi Simpson who helped structure the concept; and to all those who love Hawaii . . .

Research Notes

Tides of Change

Volcanic formation of island: Sherwin Carlquist, *Hawaii, A Natural History,* pp 5; Gavin Daws, *The Islands of Life,* pp 14.

Arrival of life: Carlquist, pp 81-101.

Adapations of flora and fauna: Ibid, pp111-190.

Warfare in old Hawaii: William Ellis, *Journal of William Ellis,* pp 113-123.

Cook's casualty figures: J.C. Beaglehole, *The Journals of Captain James Cook,* Vol. III, Part I, pp 577.

Makahiki celebration: David Malo, *Hawaiian Antiquities,* see index; John Papa Ii, Fragments of *Hawaiian History,* pp 70-7.

Cleanliness and waste disposal among Hawaiians: O. A. Bushnell, *Hygiene and Sanitation Among the Ancient Hawaiians, Hawaiian Historical Review:* Ebenezer Townsend, Diary of, *Hawaiian Historical Review,* Reprint No. 4.

Waste disposal among North American Indians: Nathaniel Portlock, *Voyage Around the World,* 1785-88, pp 284-85.

The Ocean

Number of surfing sites in Hawaii: *State of Hawaii Data Book.*

Missionaries and surfing: Hiram Bingham, *A Residence of Twenty-One Years in the Sandwich Islands,* pp 136-7.

Discovery and history of Honolulu Harbor: Bob Krauss, *Maritime Chronologies for Hawaii, Harbors.*

Semaphore ship signals: Ibid.

Boat Day: Ibid.

Container cargo figures: A. A. Smyser, *Honolulu Star-Bulletin,* Feb. 2, 1989.

Number of amateur canoe clubs: Moku Froiseth, Personal communication.

The Land

Increase in land costs in Hawaii: Krauss, *The Honolulu Advertiser,* Feb. 22, 1976; Floyd K. Takeguchi, *Star-Bulletin,* June 26, 1989.

Land ownership in old Hawaii: John H. Wise, *Ancient Hawaiian Civilization,* Chapter 7; Malo, *Hawaiian Antiquities,* see index for Land.

Place names: Mary Kawena Pukui, *Place Names of Hawaii.*

Distribution of land under the Mahele: Marion Kelly, Personal communication.

Development of Waikiki: George Vancouver, *A Voyage of Discovery,* Vol. II. pp 163-64; Barry Seichi Nakamura, *The Story of Waikiki and the "Reclamation" Project,* masters thesis.

Who Are We?

Confusion over racial definitions: Robert C. Schmitt, Personal communication; Krauss, *The Honolulu Advertiser,* June 15, 1983.

School for hapa haole girls: *Polynesian,* Mar. 21, 1846, pp 2.

Royal Hawaiian Band protest: *Pacific Commercial Advertiser,* Feb. 2, 1893, pp 3.

Kamehameha Schools attitude about the hula: Nona Beamer, Personal communication.

Statistics about numbers of part-Hawaiians: *State of Hawaii Data Book.*

Governor John Waihee on Hawaiian stew: Krauss, *The Honolulu Advertiser,* Dec. 17, 1984.

Old Gods And New Technology

Airport signs: Krauss, *The Honolulu Advertiser,* Mar. 12, 1989.

Number of cars in Hawaii, miles of roads: *State of Hawaii Data Book.*

Fireworks display and traffic gridlock: *The Honolulu Advertiser,* Jan. 8, 1989.

Attitude of Kamehameha toward new technology: Ralph Kuykendahl, *The Hawaiian Kingdom 1778-1854,* pp 65-70, 85-92.

Sugar history: Lawrence H. Fuchs, *Hawaii Pono,* see index for Sugar and Unions.

Clean technologies in Hawaii: Ronald Hayes, Personal communication.

Energy saving statistics: John Bardach, Personal communication.

How We Cope

Waikiki tourism and population density numbers: *State of Hawaii Date Book.*

Comments of Honolulu businessmen on leadership: Krauss, *The Honolulu Advertiser,* Nov. 2, 1986.

The feast: Krauss, *The Island Way,* pp 322-25.